PEARSON LANGUAGE CENTRAL
for MATH

PEARSON

Glenview, Illinois • Boston, Massachusetts • Chandler, Arizona • Upper Saddle River, New Jersey

Language Central for Math
Fitchburg Public Schools Curriculum Project Team

Principal Author
Patricia Page Aube

Contributing Authors
Grades 3–5
Lee Cormier
Amy Dessureau
Helen Frerichs
Susan Hanno
Carmelita Hoffmann
Kelly Waples McLinden
Cynthia Rosancrans
Eileen Shireman

Project Director
Bonnie Baer-Simahk

Technical Assistance
Richard Lavers

Sponsor
Massachusetts Department of Elementary
and Secondary Education's (ESE) Office
of English Language Acquisition, 2009.

Cover Art: Lorena Alvarez

ISBN-13: 978-0-13-317288-1
ISBN-10: 0-13-317288-0

3 4 5 6 7 8 9 10 V063 15 14 13

How to Use
Language Central for Math

This book will help you **think, talk,** and **write** about what you are learning in your math class. Every lesson has 4 pages to help you learn the language needed to succeed in math.

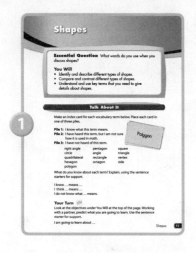

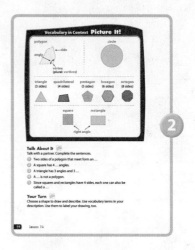

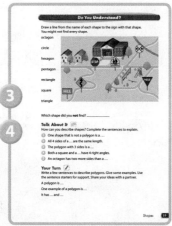

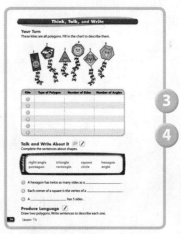

1. Activities connect what you know with what you will learn.
   Look for the **blue bar** on the first page.

2. Vocabulary terms are shown with pictures to help you learn what they mean.
   Look for the **red box** on the second page.

3. Look for clues to help you know when to write an answer 🖉 and when to speak an answer 💬.

4. Practice the skills you learn in your math class.

CONTENTS

Grade 3

Lesson 1: Place Value 1

Lesson 2: Comparing Numbers 5

Lesson 3: Addition and Subtraction 9

Lesson 4: Meaning of Multiplication 13

Lesson 5: Multiplication and Division Facts 17

Lesson 6: Understanding Story Problems 21

Lesson 7: Estimation 25

Lesson 8: Fractions 29

Lesson 9: Fractions on a Number Line 33

Lesson 10: Number Sentences 37

Lesson 11: Patterns 41

Lesson 12: Lines 45

Lesson 13: Angles 49

Lesson 14: Shapes 53

Lesson 15: Triangles and Quadrilaterals 57

Lesson 16: Figures in Our World 61

Lesson 17: Units of Measure 65

Lesson 18: Measurement Tools 69

Lesson 19: Perimeter and Area 73

Lesson 20: Time 77

Lesson 21: Collecting and Organizing Data 81

Lesson 22: Representing Data 85

Resources 89

Place Value

Essential Question What do you need to know to understand and discuss place value in math class?

You Will
- Identify place value in numbers through 9,999.
- Represent numbers using standard form, expanded form, and word form.
- Use key terms to talk about numbers.

Talk About It

Rate these mathematical terms according to the following scale:

1 I have never heard of this term before.

2 I have heard this term, but I do not know how to use it in math.

3 I understand this term and know how to use it in math.

_____ digits	_____ tens
_____ numbers	_____ hundreds
_____ place value	_____ thousands
_____ ones	_____ standard form
_____ place	_____ expanded form
_____ value	_____ word form

Explain what you know about these terms, using the sentence starters.

I do not know what … means.
I think … means …
I know … means … in math.

Your Turn

Look at the objectives listed under You Will at the top of the page. Working with a partner, predict what you will learn. Use the sentence starter for help.

I will learn about …

digits

0 1 2 3 4 5 6 7 8 9

standard form

1,392

numbers

14   9   570   1,392

expanded form

1,000 + 300 + 90 + 2

place value

The 3 is in the hundreds **place.**
The **value** of the 3 is 300.

word form

one thousand, three hundred ninety-two

Talk About It

Talk with a partner. Complete the sentences.

1. The number 4,876 is written in …

2. In the number 4,876, the 4, 8, 7, and 6 are all …

3. In the number 2,598, the 5 is in the …

4. 5,000 + 100 + 20 + 6 is written in …

5. In the number 8,764, the … of the 8 is 8,000.

Your Turn

Write a four-digit number. Tell how to read the number. Then use the vocabulary terms to describe the number in different ways to a partner.

Tallest Mountain on Each Continent

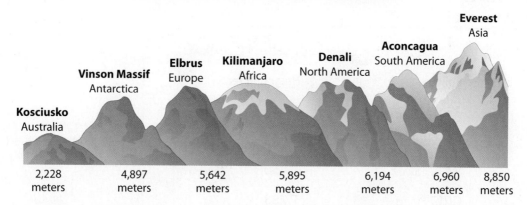

Kosciusko Australia	Vinson Massif Antarctica	Elbrus Europe	Kilimanjaro Africa	Denali North America	Aconcagua South America	Everest Asia
2,228 meters	4,897 meters	5,642 meters	5,895 meters	6,194 meters	6,960 meters	8,850 meters

Write the numbers for the heights in the table below. Use standard and expanded form.

Mountain Heights		
Mountain	**Standard Form**	**Expanded Form**
Everest	8,850	8,000 + 800 + 50

Talk About It

How can you represent numbers? Complete the sentences to explain.

1. In standard notation, you write the number using …

2. In expanded notation, you show the … of each digit.

Your Turn

Look at this number: 4,312. Describe this number to a partner using vocabulary terms.

Think, Talk, and Write

Your Turn

Look at the table.

Some of the World's Tallest Buildings	
Building	**Height (in feet)**
Taipei 101 Tower	1,667
Petronas Towers	1,483
Willis Tower	1,450
CITIC Plaza	1,283
Empire State Building	1,250

Choose one building. Describe its height in three different ways.

Building: _____

Height in standard form: _____

Height in expanded form: _____

Height in word form: _____

Talk and Write About It

Complete the sentences about the building you chose.

Vocabulary			
digits	thousands	ones	standard form
numbers	hundreds	value	expanded form
place value	tens	place	word form

1. The height of the building is a number with four _____ .

2. The digit 1 is in the _____ place.

3. The heights in the table are in _____ .

Produce Language

Write about the different forms for representing numbers. Try using all the terms you rated with a 1 or 2 on the first page of the lesson.

Comparing Numbers

Essential Question How do you use words and symbols
(<, >, =) to compare numbers?

You Will
- Use the symbols <, >, and = to compare numbers.
- Use math vocabulary to compare numbers.

Talk About It

Tear out the Comparing Schools Four Corners Activity sheet on
pages 91–92. Then cut out the activity cards on page 93.

Work with a partner.

Each corner of the room shows a school and the number of students at
that school.

Step 1 Go to a corner of the room. On the activity sheet, write the
name of the school and the number of students in one of
the boxes.

Step 2 Follow the directions in the box. Paste the correct card in
the box.

Repeat Steps 1 and 2 for each corner of the room.

Look at the red terms in each box. What do you know about these
terms? Use the sentence starters for support.

I know … means …
I think … means …
I do not know what … means.

Your Turn

Look at the objectives listed under You Will at the top of the page.
Working with a partner, predict what you will learn. Use the sentence
starter below.

I am going to learn about …

compare Tell how things are the same or different.

. . . .

equals The same amount as

●●●●●●●●   ●●●●●●●●
●●●●●●●●   ●●●●●●●●

12 + 4	**equals**	16.
12 + 4	**is equal to**	16.
12 + 4	=	16

greater Bigger

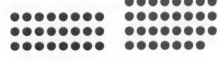

15 is greater than 13.

15   >   13

. . . .

less Smaller

●●●●●●●●   ●●●●●●●●
●●●●●●●●   ●●●●●●●●
●●●●●●●●   ●●●●●●●●

24   is less than   31.

24   <   31

. . . .

symbols

=   >   <

Talk About It

Talk with a partner to complete these sentences.

1. 29 … 25.

2. 40 plus 40 … 80.

3. 20 < 60 means twenty … sixty.

4. 171 > 112 means one hundred seventy-one … one hundred twelve.

Your Turn

Share your Four Corners activity sheet with a partner. Talk about how you compared the numbers. Use the terms on this page.

You can use words and symbols to compare the number of students in Grade 5 to the number of students in Grade 3.

Words: 94 is less than 121.

Symbols: 94 < 121

Grade 3: 121 students
Grade 4: 109 students
Grade 5: 94 students
Grade 6: 109 students

1 Compare the number of students in Grade 6 to the number of students in Grade 3.

Words: 109 _____ 121.

Symbols: 109 ☐ 121

2 Compare the number of students in Grade 4 to the number of students in Grade 6.

Words: 109 _____ 109.

Symbols: 109 ☐ 109

3 Compare the number of students in Grade 6 to the number of students in Grade 5.

Words: 109 _____ 94.

Symbols: 109 ☐ 94

Talk About It

What words and symbols can you use to compare numbers? Complete the sentences to explain.

4 The symbol > means …

5 The symbol < means …

6 The symbol = means …

Your Turn

Pick any two numbers in the box at the right. Tell your partner how the two numbers compare.

41   193
  68   400
193   255

Think, Talk, and Write

Your Turn

Circle the words to compare the numbers.

1
    is greater than

84   is equal to   127

    is less than

2
    is greater than

141   is equal to   114

    is less than

3
    is greater than

309   is equal to   309

    is less than

4
    is greater than

513   is equal to   489

    is less than

Circle the symbol to compare the numbers.

5
    $>$

74   $=$ 74

    $<$

6
    $>$

565   $=$ 333

    $<$

7
    $>$

70   $=$ 700

    $<$

Talk and Write About It

Complete each sentence about comparing numbers.

Vocabulary		
compare	greater	less
equals	is greater than, $>$	is less than, $<$
is equal to, $=$	symbols	

8 If two numbers are the same, use the symbol _____ .

9 If the first number is greater than the second number, use the symbol _____ .

10 If the first number is less than the second number, use the symbol _____ .

Produce Language

Write about what you have learned about comparing numbers. You may include examples. Use as many vocabulary terms and symbols as you can.

Addition and Subtraction

Essential Question What words and symbols do you need to know in order to learn about addition and subtraction?

You Will
- Add 2-digit and 3-digit numbers.
- Subtract 2-digit and 3-digit numbers.
- Use key terms to describe addition and subtraction.

Talk About It

Copy each term from Vocabulary in Context on a card. Listen to your teacher read each term. Create three piles of cards.

1 Place terms that you know in **Pile 1.**

2 Place terms you have heard but are not sure what they mean in **Pile 2.**

3 Place terms you do not know in **Pile 3.**

What do you know about each term? Explain. Use the sentence starters for support.

I know … means …
I think … means …
I do not know what … means.

Your Turn

Look at the objectives listed under You Will at the top of the page. Working with a partner, predict what you will learn. Use the sentence starter below.

I am going to learn about …

plus

difference

regroup

add

addition sentence: 6 + 2 = 8

↑ equals

plus

$$\begin{array}{r} 6 \\ + 2 \\ \hline 8 \end{array}$$

← addends
← sum

subtract

subtraction sentence: 6 − 2 = 4

minus

$$\begin{array}{r} 6 \\ - 2 \\ \hline 4 \end{array}$$

← difference

place value

thousands	hundreds	tens	ones
1,	3	9	2

symbols + − =

regroup

$$\begin{array}{r} \overset{1}{4}\,7 \\ + 3\,8 \\ \hline 8\,5 \end{array}$$

15 ones = 1 ten 5 ones

$$\begin{array}{r} \overset{8\ 12}{\cancel{9}\,\cancel{2}} \\ - 1\,7 \\ \hline 7\,5 \end{array}$$

9 tens 2 ones = 8 tens 12 ones

Talk About It

Talk with a partner. Complete the sentences.

1. Use + to do …

2. Use − to do …

3. Add numbers to find the …

4. Subtract numbers to find the …

5. When subtracting, sometimes you cannot subtract the ones, so you need to …

Your Turn

Write an addition sentence. Write a subtraction sentence. Talk about the parts of each sentence with a partner. Use all the vocabulary terms you can.

Complete the cards.

Bridal Veil Falls

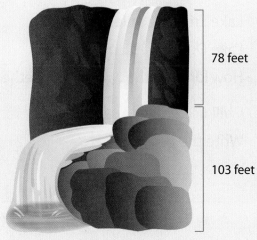

78 feet

103 feet

How many feet high is Bridal Veil Falls?

Write the problem:

$$\begin{array}{r} 78 \\ +103 \\ \hline \end{array}$$

The waterfall is _____ feet high.

Statue of Liberty

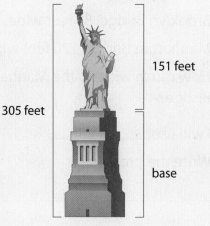

151 feet

305 feet

base

How many feet high is the base?

Write the problem:

The base is _____ feet high.

Talk About It

How did you solve the problems? Complete the sentences to explain.

1 For the Bridal Veil Falls problem, I used …

2 For the Statue of Liberty problem, I used …

3 To add the numbers, I started with the … digit.

4 When subtracting, I had to …

Your Turn

Choose two numbers and one symbol from the box at the right. Write and solve a problem. Tell your partner about the problem.

+	−	567
94		830

Think, Talk, and Write

Your Turn
Complete the cards.

Brooklyn Bridge: 85 feet wide

Manhattan Bridge: 120 feet wide

How much wider is the Manhattan Bridge?

I will use _____ .

Write the problem:

It is _____ feet wider.

Lake Erie: 241 miles long

Lake Ontario: 193 miles long

How long are the two lakes together?

I will use _____ .

Write the problem:

Together, the lakes are _____ miles long.

Talk and Write About It
Complete the sentences about the problems.

Vocabulary

addition	minus	subtraction	difference
plus	sum	equals	addends

1. To solve the bridge problem, I used _____ .

2. I had to find the _____ between the widths of the two bridges.

3. The answer to the lake problem is a _____ .

Produce Language
Write about how you used regrouping to solve one problem. Use the vocabulary terms.

Meaning of Multiplication

Essential Question What vocabulary terms do you need to use when you discuss multiplication?

You Will
- Model, write, and solve multiplication problems.
- Learn about odd numbers, even numbers, and multiples.
- Use key terms to talk about multiplication.

Talk About It

Make an index card for each vocabulary term below. Place each card in one of three piles.

1. Place terms that you know in **Pile 1.**

2. Place terms you have heard but are not sure what they mean in **Pile 2.**

multiples

3. Place terms you do not know in **Pile 3.**

factors	product	array
multiples	even numbers	column
multiplication	odd numbers	row
multiply	times	

What do you know about each term? Explain, using the sentence starters for support.

I know … means …
I think … means …
I do not know what … means.

Your Turn

Look at the objectives listed under You Will at the top of the page. Working with a partner, predict what you will learn. Use the sentence starter below.

I am going to learn about …

multiply

$$\begin{array}{r} 2 \\ \times\ 4 \\ \hline 8 \end{array}$$

times → $\times 4$ > **factors**

product

array

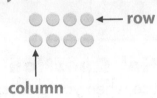

← **row**

↑
column

2 (rows) × 4 (columns) = 8

multiplication sentence

2 × 4 = 8

even numbers

2, 4, 6, 8, 10, …

odd numbers

1, 3, 5, 7, 9, …

multiples of 4

4, 8, 12, 16, …

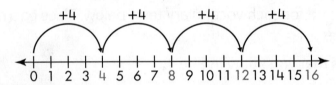

+4   +4   +4   +4

0 1 2 3 4 5 6 7 8 9 10 11 12 13 14 15 16

Talk About It

Talk with a partner. Complete the sentences.

1 The numbers you multiply are called …

2 The answer to a multiplication problem is the …

3 1, 3, and 5 are …

4 All multiples of 2 are also …

5 6 × 4 = 24 is a … sentence.

Your Turn

Look at the array in the chart above. How can you describe it?
Use as many vocabulary terms as possible. Tell a partner.

The tiled floors of three rooms are pictured below. Complete the multiplication sentences to find the number of tiles in each room.

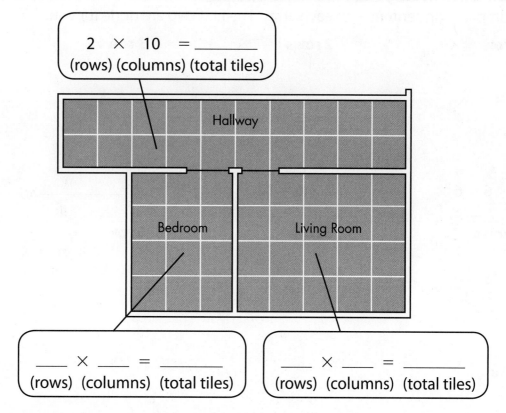

2 × 10 = _____
(rows) (columns) (total tiles)

Hallway

Bedroom

Living Room

____ × ____ = _____
(rows) (columns) (total tiles)

____ × ____ = _____
(rows) (columns) (total tiles)

Talk About It

How does multiplication work? Complete the sentences to explain.

1. One way to picture multiplication is with an …

2. The number of rows and the number of columns in the array are the …

3. The total number in the array is the …

Your Turn

Write a multiplication sentence. Explain it to a partner. Use the sentence starters for support.

The factors are …

The product is …

Your Turn

Draw different arrays that each have 6 columns. Write the multiplication sentence for each array. The first two are done for you.

1 row

2 rows

3 rows

$1 \times 6 = 6$ $2 \times 6 = 12$ _____

4 rows   **5 rows**   **6 rows**

_____   _____   _____

Talk and Write About It

Complete the sentences about the multiplication sentences you wrote.

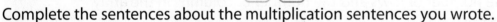

Vocabulary			
multiples	factor	odd number	even number
multiply	product	array	column

1. All of the multiplication sentences have 6 as a _____ .

2. The products 6, 12, 18, 24, 30, and 36 are all _____ of 6.

3. In the multiplication sentence $3 \times 6 = 18$, there are two even numbers and one _____ .

Produce Language

Write about factors, multiples, and multiplication sentences. Use your vocabulary cards for support.

Multiplication and Division Facts

Essential Question What words and symbols should you use when you learn about multiplication and division facts?

You Will
- Write multiplication and division facts.
- Learn about multiplication and division fact families.
- Use key terms to talk about multiplication and division.

Talk About It

Look at the list of terms below. In the first two columns of the chart, write terms you **know** or **want** to know more about.

array	division fact	multiply
column	divisor	product
divide	fact family	quotient
divided by	factor	row
dividend	multiplication fact	times

Know	Want	Learned

What do you know about each term you wrote in the chart? Explain, using the sentence starters for support.

I know … means …
I want to know more about …

Your Turn
Look at the objectives under You Will at the top of the page. Working with a partner, predict what you are going to learn. Use the sentence starter for support.

I am going to learn about …

Vocabulary in Context Picture It!

multiply   **times**

$$4 \times 6 = 24$$

factors **product**

....

divide   **divided by**

$$24 \div 6 = 4$$

dividend **divisor** **quotient**

array

●●●●●●● ←— **row**
●●●●●●
●●●●●●
●●●●●●

column

4 (rows) $\times$ 6 (columns) $= 24$
$24 \div 4$ (rows) $= 6$ (columns)

....

fact family

$$4 \times 6 = 24$$
$$6 \times 4 = 24$$ **multiplication facts**
$$24 \div 6 = 4$$
$$24 \div 4 = 6$$ **division facts**

Talk About It

Talk with a partner. Complete the sentences.

1. To find a product, multiply the …

2. The symbol $\div$ means …

3. The answer to a division problem is the …

4. $2 \times 8 = 16$ and $16 \div 8 = 2$ belong to the same …

5. An array is made up of rows and …

Your Turn

Look at the fact family shown in the chart above. How can you describe it? Use as many vocabulary terms as possible. Tell a partner.

Look at two ways a marching band can line up. Complete the fact family for each array.

Fact Family

$$4 \quad \times \quad 3 \quad = \quad 12$$

$$\underline{\hspace{2cm}} \times \underline{\hspace{2cm}} = \underline{\hspace{2cm}}$$

$$\underline{\hspace{2cm}} \div \underline{\hspace{2cm}} = \underline{\hspace{2cm}}$$

$$12 \quad \div \quad 3 \quad = \quad 4$$

Fact Family

$$\underline{\hspace{2cm}} \times \underline{\hspace{2cm}} = \underline{\hspace{2cm}}$$

$$\underline{\hspace{2cm}} \times \underline{\hspace{2cm}} = \underline{\hspace{2cm}}$$

$$\underline{\hspace{2cm}} \div \underline{\hspace{2cm}} = \underline{\hspace{2cm}}$$

$$\underline{\hspace{2cm}} \div \underline{\hspace{2cm}} = \underline{\hspace{2cm}}$$

Talk About It

What terms help you to understand multiplication and division facts? Complete the sentences to explain.

1. There are usually four facts in a …

2. In a division fact, the number you are dividing by is the …

3. In a multiplication fact, the numbers being multiplied are the …

Your Turn

Write a division fact that belongs in the fact family for $9 \times 3 = 27$. Write how the facts are related. Share with a partner.

Your Turn

Draw an array with 9 rows and 4 columns.
Then write the fact family that goes with the array.

Array   **Fact Family**

_____

_____

_____

_____

Talk and Write About It

Complete the sentences about the array and the fact family.

Vocabulary			
dividend	factors	quotient	fact families
product	times	divisor	array

1. In each division fact, 36 is the _____ .

2. In each multiplication fact, 36 is the _____ .

3. The number of rows and the number of columns in my array are

    the _____ in the multiplication facts.

Produce Language

Write the terms you learned about in this lesson in the third column
of the chart on page 17. Write what you know about these terms.
Use sentence starters from throughout the lesson for support.

Understanding Story Problems

Essential Question What words do you need to understand when you solve story problems?

You Will

- Read story problems and choose the right operation to solve them.
- Use all four operations to solve story problems.
- Use key vocabulary terms to discuss story problems and how to solve them.

Talk About It

Rate these mathematical terms according to the following scale.

① I have never heard of this term before.

② I have heard this term, but I do not know how to use it in math.

③ I understand this term and know how to use it in math.

_____ addition	_____ multiplication	_____ subtraction
_____ difference	_____ plus	_____ sum
_____ division	_____ product	_____ times
_____ divided by	_____ quotient	_____ operations
_____ minus	_____ remainder	

What do you know about each term? Explain, using the sentence starters for support.

I do not know what … means.
I think … means …
I know … means …

Your Turn

Look at the objectives listed under You Will at the top of the page. Working with a partner, predict what you will learn. Use the sentence starter below.

I am going to learn about …

add  subtract

addition sentence: $8 + 2 = 10$

plus   sum

subtraction sentence: $6 - 2 = 4$

minus

difference

multiply  **multiplication** sentence:

$4 \times 3 = 12$

times

product

divide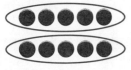

division sentence:

$10 \div 5 = 2$

divided by

quotient

$$5\overline{)11}\;\;^{2R1}$$

remainder

operations $+ \; - \; \times \; \div$

Talk About It

Talk with a partner. Complete the sentences. Look at the diagrams for help.

1. To put things together, use …

2. To take away some things, use …

3. If things are in equal groups, you can find the total number by using …

4. To split things into equal groups, use …

5. The amount left over when you divide is called the …

Your Turn

Look at the operations and symbols above. How can you describe them? Use as many vocabulary terms as possible. Tell a partner.

Read the problem. Draw a picture. The first picture is drawn for you.
Then complete the number sentence to find the answer.

Addition

Jenny feeds 12 goats and 5 cows. How many animals does she feed?

_____ + _____ = _____ animals

Subtraction

The chickens laid 22 eggs. The ducks laid 16 eggs. How many more eggs did the chickens lay?

_____ − _____ = _____ more eggs

Multiplication

Rico has 7 horses. Each horse has 4 horseshoes. How many horseshoes are there?

_____ × _____ = _____ horseshoes

Division

Ben has 30 pigs. He puts 6 pigs in each pen. How many pens will be filled with pigs?

_____ ÷ _____ = _____ pens

Talk About It

Complete the sentences to tell about the problems.

1. In a number sentence, + stands for the word …

2. The answer to a subtraction problem is called the …

3. The product is the answer to a … problem.

4. If there had been any pigs left over in the division problem, the number of pigs left over would be called the …

Your Turn

Use one of the stories on this page as a model to write a story problem. Solve the problem. Tell your partner about the problem.

Your Turn

Write a number sentence to solve the problem. Then give the answer to the problem.

1. Julia fills 10 bags with cherries. She puts 5 cherries in a bag. How many cherries does Julia have in all?

    Number sentence: _____

    Julia has _____ cherries.

2. There are 45 pumpkins in one patch and 38 pumpkins in another patch. How many pumpkins are there in all?

    Number sentence: _____

    There are _____ pumpkins in all.

3. Camilla grew 16 tomatoes. She gives them to 4 friends. Each friend gets the same number. How many tomatoes does she give to each friend?

    Number sentence: _____

    Each friend gets _____ tomatoes.

Talk and Write About It

Complete the sentences about the story problems you solved.

Vocabulary			
addition	product	subtract	multiplication
remainder	sum	divide	operations

4. In Problem 1, I used _____ .

5. In Problem 2, I found the _____ .

6. In Problem 3, I needed to _____ .

Produce Language

Write about the steps you used to solve one of the problems. Use vocabulary terms in your sentences.

Estimation

You Will
- Apply what you know about numbers and operations to estimate answers to math problems.
- Use rounding to help you make good estimates.
- Understand and use key terms related to estimation.

Talk About It

Make an index card for each vocabulary term below. Place each card in one of three piles.

Pile 1: I know what this term means.
Pile 2: I have heard of this term, but I am not sure how it is used in math.
Pile 3: I have not heard of this term.

estimate

exactly	round	estimate
reasonable	nearest ten	about
unreasonable		

What do you know about each term? Explain, using the sentence starters for support.

I know … means …
I think … means …
I do not know what … means.

Your Turn

Look at the objectives under You Will at the top of the page. Working with a partner, predict what you are going to learn. Use the sentence starter for support.

I am going to learn about …

exactly 287 marbles
about 300 marbles

reasonable guess: 600 marbles
unreasonable guess: 6,000 marbles

round Replace one number with another number that is about the same amount.

67 → 70
nearest ten

67

60   70   80

estimate Tell about how much.

An **estimate** is a good guess.

Talk About It

Talk with a partner. Complete the sentences.

1. A logical guess is an ...

2. When you round 32 to 30, you round it to the ...

3. There are ... 24 hours in a day.

4. An estimate of 100 days in a month is ...

Your Turn

Choose three terms from the chart above. Use your own words to tell your partner what each term means.

It's time for the Fourth of July parade! Read the story problems. Then fill in the missing numbers to find the estimates.

1 A clown has 72 balloons. He gives away 48. About how many balloons are left?

Round 72 to the nearest ten: _____

Round 48 to the nearest ten: _____

Subtract: _____ − _____ = _____

Estimate: about _____ balloons

2 Last year there were 11 floats in the parade. This year there will be 3 times as many. About how many floats will there be?

Round 11 to the nearest ten: _____

Multiply: _____ × _____ = _____

Estimate: about _____ floats

3 Use the table. About how many band members are there in all?

Round 57 to the nearest ten: _____

Round 45 to the nearest ten: _____

Round 83 to the nearest ten: _____

Add: _____ + _____ + _____ = _____

Estimate: about _____ band members

Band	Marching Band Members
A	57
B	45
C	83

Talk About It

Complete the sentences about these problems.

4 I rounded the numbers to the ...

5 I computed with rounded numbers to find an ...

6 My estimated answer tells ... how many.

Your Turn

Write a story problem and estimate the answer. Share your story problem with a partner. Tell how you estimated the answer.

Your Turn

Use rounding to find each estimate. Show your work.

1 About how many beef tacos and chicken tacos are there in all?

Paul's Taco Stand	
Taco	**Number**
Beef	31
Chicken	65
Fish	42
Bean	28
Cheese	17

About _____ beef and chicken tacos

2 About how many more fish tacos are there than bean tacos?

About _____ more fish tacos

3 Yesterday, there were 4 times as many cheese tacos. About how many cheese tacos were there yesterday?

About _____ cheese tacos

Talk and Write About It

Complete the sentences.

Vocabulary

| about | round | exactly | unreasonable |
| estimate | nearest ten | reasonable | |

4 I estimated by rounding numbers to the _____ .

5 When I round the numbers in a problem, the answer is an _____ .

6 If my estimate is close to the exact amount, my estimate is _____ .

Produce Language

Write about how rounding and estimating are related. Use an example. Use vocabulary terms in your sentences.

Fractions

Essential Question What words do you need to understand when you discuss fractions?

You Will
- Identify and show fractions using figures, numbers, and terms.
- Understand and use key terms related to fractions.

Talk About It

Look at the list of terms below. In the first two columns of the chart, write terms you **know** or **want** to know more about.

equal parts	whole	fifth	fifths
fraction	half	halves	sixth
numerator	third	thirds	sixths
denominator	fourth	fourths	

Know	Want	Learned

What do you know about each term? Explain, using the sentence starters for support.

I know … means …
I want to know more about …

Your Turn

Look at the objectives under You Will at the top of the page. Working with a partner, predict what you are going to learn. Use the sentence starter for support.

I am going to learn about …

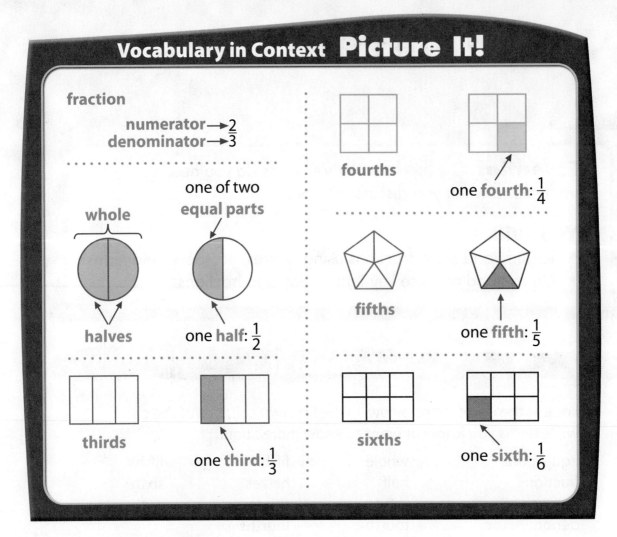

fraction

numerator→$\frac{2}{3}$
denominator→$\frac{2}{3}$

whole — **one of two equal parts**

halves — **one half:** $\frac{1}{2}$

thirds — **one third:** $\frac{1}{3}$

fourths — **one fourth:** $\frac{1}{4}$

fifths — **one fifth:** $\frac{1}{5}$

sixths — **one sixth:** $\frac{1}{6}$

Talk About It

Talk with a partner. Complete the sentences.

1. A fraction names a part of a …

2. One whole can be divided into …

3. The total number of equal parts is the … of the fraction.

4. A whole can be divided into three …

5. In the fraction $\frac{4}{5}$, the 4 is the …

Your Turn

Describe one of the fractions in the box. Use as many vocabulary terms as you can. Tell a partner.

$$\frac{2}{3} \quad \frac{1}{4} \quad \frac{2}{6} \quad \frac{4}{5}$$

Look at the flower garden below. It is divided into 5 equal parts. Write the fraction of the garden that has blue flowers and the fraction that has pink flowers. Use the numbers for the part that has white flowers as a model.

There are 5 equal parts.

One part of the garden has white flowers.

$\frac{1}{5}$ of the garden has white flowers.

Blue flowers:

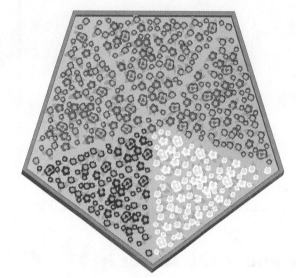

Pink flowers:

Talk About It

How can you describe the garden? Complete the sentences.

1. The garden is divided into five …
2. Each part is one … of the garden.
3. Each fraction of flowers in the garden has 5 in the …

Your Turn

Choose one of the ways shown below to divide a garden that is shaped like a rectangle. How would you describe it? Use the sentence starters for support. Share your ideas with a partner.

This garden is divided into …
The fraction … represents one part of this garden.

Your Turn

Draw a vegetable garden divided into 6 equal parts. Color 3 parts yellow for corn, color 2 parts red for tomatoes, and color 1 part green for peas. Write the fraction of the garden planted with each type of vegetable.

The fraction of the garden that has corn is

_____ .

The fraction of the garden that has tomatoes is

_____ .

The fraction of the garden that has peas is

_____ .

Talk and Write About It

Complete the sentences about the garden.

Vocabulary			
equal parts	sixth	thirds	fraction
fourth	whole	half	numerator

1. Peas are planted in one _____ of the garden.

2. All the parts for corn, tomatoes, and peas make up the

   _____ garden.

3. Each type of vegetable is a different _____ of the garden.

4. Before I colored the garden, I divided it into six _____ .

Produce Language

Write the terms you learned about in this lesson in the third column of the chart on page 29. Write what you have learned about these terms. Use sentence starters from throughout the lesson for support.

Fractions on a Number Line

> **Essential Question** How do you use vocabulary terms to describe fractions on a number line?

> **You Will**
> - Identify fractions and mixed numbers.
> - Use a number line to compare fractions and mixed numbers.
> - Use math terms to discuss fractions, mixed numbers, and number lines.

Talk About It

Copy each term from Vocabulary in Context on a card. As your teacher reads each term, create three piles of cards.

1. Place terms that you know in **Pile 1.**

2. Place terms you have heard but are not sure what they mean in **Pile 2.**

3. Place terms you do not know in **Pile 3.**

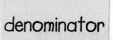

denominator	is greater than	numerator
equal parts	is less than	number line
fraction	mixed number	tick mark

What do you know about each term? Explain, using the sentence starters for support.

I know … means …
I think … means …
I do not know what … means.

Your Turn

Look at the objectives under You Will at the top of the page. Working with a partner, predict what you are going to learn. Use the sentence starter for support.

I am going to learn about …

fraction

$\frac{1}{2}$ ←numerator
←denominator

mixed number

whole number →$1\frac{1}{4}$← fraction

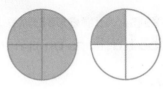

number line

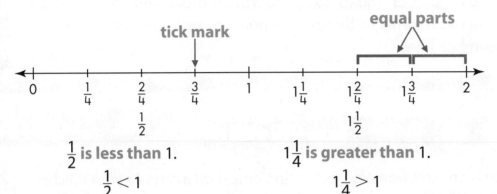

tick mark

equal parts

0    $\frac{1}{4}$ $\frac{2}{4}$ $\frac{3}{4}$ 1 $1\frac{1}{4}$ $1\frac{2}{4}$ $1\frac{3}{4}$ 2

$\frac{1}{2}$ $1\frac{1}{2}$

$\frac{1}{2}$ is less than 1. $1\frac{1}{4}$ is greater than 1.

$\frac{1}{2} < 1$ $1\frac{1}{4} > 1$

Talk About It

Talk with a partner. Complete the sentences.

1. The top number in a fraction is the …

2. The bottom number in a fraction is the …

3. Every mixed number … 1.

4. By looking at a number line, I see that $\frac{1}{4}$ … $\frac{1}{2}$.

5. Tick marks show how a number line is divided into …

Your Turn

Write a mixed number. Describe it to a partner. Use the sentence starters if you need help.

The whole number in my mixed number is …

The fraction in my mixed number is …

The numerator is …

The denominator is …

It is greater than …

The number line shows how many miles it is from Lola's house to other places.

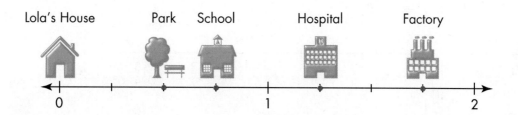

Write how far each place is from Lola's house.

Park: _____ mile

Hospital: _____ miles

School: _____ mile

Factory: _____ miles

Talk About It

Complete the sentences about the distances on the number line.

1. Between 0 and 1, the number line is divided into four …

2. The number I wrote for the distance to the factory is a …

3. The fraction $\frac{1}{2}$ is … $\frac{3}{4}$.

4. $1\frac{3}{4}$ … $1\frac{1}{4}$.

Your Turn

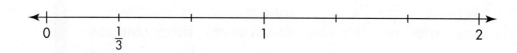

Fill in the number line with fractions and mixed numbers. Use the sentence starters to tell a partner what you did.

The number line is divided into …

I wrote the fraction …

I wrote the mixed numbers …

Use the number lines to answer the questions.

1. Circle $\frac{1}{4}$ and $\frac{1}{3}$ on the number lines.

   Is $\frac{1}{4}$ greater than $\frac{1}{3}$ or less than $\frac{1}{3}$?

   _____

2. Circle $1\frac{1}{2}$ and $1\frac{3}{4}$ on the blue number line.

   Is $1\frac{3}{4}$ greater than $1\frac{1}{2}$ or less than $1\frac{1}{2}$?

   _____

3. Circle $1\frac{1}{3}$ on the green number line.

   What kind of number is $1\frac{1}{3}$?

   _____

Talk and Write About It

Complete the sentences.

Vocabulary

| denominator | fractions | numerator | is less than |
| is greater than | number line | equal parts | mixed numbers |

4. The numbers shown on the number line between 0 and 1 are

   _____ .

5. The numbers shown on the number line between 1 and 2 are

   _____ .

6. In the fraction $\frac{1}{3}$, the 3 is the _____ .

Produce Language

Write how a number line can help you describe fractions and mixed numbers. Use examples and your vocabulary cards for support.

Number Sentences

Essential Question What vocabulary do you need to discuss number sentences?

You Will
- Identify four types of number sentences: addition, subtraction, multiplication, division.
- Find the value of a missing number in a number sentence.
- Understand and use key terms when discussing and solving number sentences.

Talk About It

Rate these mathematical terms according to the following scale.

1 I have never heard of this term.

2 I have heard this term, but I do not know how to use it in math.

3 I understand this term and know how to use it in math.

_____ addition sentence   _____ multiplication sentence
_____ division sentence   _____ number sentences
_____ equation   _____ subtraction sentence
_____ missing number   _____ value

What do you know about each term? Explain, using the sentence starters for support.

I do not know what … means.
I think … means …
I know … means …

Your Turn
Look at the objectives under You Will at the top of the page. Working with a partner, predict what you are going to learn. Use the sentence starter for support.

I am going to learn about …

number sentences

addition
sentence   11 + 4 = 15

· ·

subtraction
sentence   15 − 11 = 4

· ·

multiplication
sentence   4 × 3 = 12

· ·

division
sentence   12 ÷ 4 = 3

An **equation** has an equal
sign.

$$4 + 8 = 12$$
$$18 - 9 = 9$$
$$5 \times 6 = 30$$
$$16 \div 2 = 8$$

missing number

$$7 + \square = 12$$

The **value** of $\square$ is 5.

Talk About It

Talk with a partner. Complete the sentences.

1. The ÷ symbol is used in a …

2. The number sentences on this page can also be called …

3. The equation 35 − 5 = 30 is a …

4. In the number sentence $\triangle$ × 10 = 30, the triangle stands for a …

5. In the number sentence 5 + $\square$ = 7, the … of the square is 2.

Your Turn

Write a number sentence. How can you describe it? Use as many
vocabulary terms as possible. Tell a partner.

Ken sells fruit at his fruit stand. Write the missing numbers in the number sentences about Ken's fruit stand.

1 Ken starts with 27 oranges.
He sells most of them.
There are 6 left.
How many oranges did he sell?

$27 - \boxed{} = 6$

The missing number is _____ .

Ken sold _____ oranges.

2 Ken sells 4 bags of apples.
Each bag has the same number of apples.
He sells 40 apples in all.
How many apples are in each bag?

$4 \times \boxed{} = 40$

The value of $\boxed{}$ is _____ .

There are _____ apples in each bag.

Write the missing numbers in the box.

3 $12 \div \boxed{} = 2$

4 $\boxed{} + 24 = 32$

Talk About It

What operations and symbols help you understand number sentences? Complete the sentences to explain.

5 The 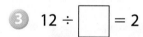 in a number sentence stands for a ...

6 In Problem 1, I completed a ...

7 In Problem 2, I completed a ...

Your Turn

Choose one number sentence from above. Write a few sentences about it. Use the sentence starters for support. Share your sentences with a partner.

The number sentence I chose is ...

The value of ...

Draw a line to match each problem to a number sentence on the right.
Then find the missing number.

1 There are 24 mangos.
Jen divides them into groups.
There are 8 mangos in each group.

Number Sentences

$\boxed{} - 24 = 4$

2 Enrique has some bananas.
He buys 8 more.
Now he has 24 bananas in all.

$4 \times \boxed{} = 24$

3 Amy has some berries.
She gives away 24 berries.
There are 4 berries left.

$24 \div \boxed{} = 8$

4 There are 4 buckets.
Each bucket has the same
number of apples in it.
There are 24 apples in all.

$\boxed{} + 8 = 24$

Talk and Write About It

Complete the sentences about the number sentences.

Vocabulary	
addition sentence	division sentence
multiplication sentence	subtraction sentence
missing number	value
equation	number sentence

5 The first problem above matches a _____ .

6 To complete each number sentence, I found the _____
of the square.

7 The + symbol is used in the _____ .

8 A number sentence can also be called an _____ .

Produce Language

Write about finding the value of a missing number in a number
sentence. Use an example. Use vocabulary terms in your sentences.

Patterns

Essential Question What vocabulary will help you explain patterns?

You Will
- Identify and continue patterns.
- Find the rule for number patterns.
- Understand and use key terms related to patterns.

Talk About It

Look at the list of terms below. In the first two columns of the chart, write terms you **know** or **want** to know more about.

pattern   number pattern   repeat
repeating pattern   rule   table

Know	Want	Learned

What do you know about each term you wrote in the chart?
Explain, using the sentence starters for support.

I know … means …
I want to know more about …

Your Turn

Look at the objectives under You Will at the top of the page. Working with a partner, predict what you are going to learn. Use the sentence starter for support.

I am going to learn about …

Vocabulary in Context **Picture It!**

patterns

repeating patterns

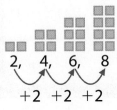

repeat

1, 2, 3, 1, 2, 3, 1, 2, 3

number patterns

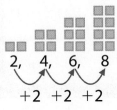

2, 4, 6, 8

+2 +2 +2

rule: add 2

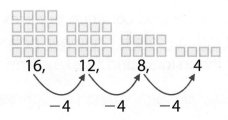

16, 12, 8, 4

−4 −4 −4

rule: subtract 4

table

Dan's Age (years)	4	5	6	7	8
Clara's Age (years)	9	10	11	12	13

rule: add 5

Talk About It

Talk with a partner. Complete the sentences.

1. 1, 3, 5, 7 is an example of a …

2. In the pattern A B A B A B A B, the letters A and B …

3. In the pattern 3, 5, 7, 9, "add 2" is the …

4. Dan's and Clara's ages are shown in a …

Your Turn

Look at the pattern below. Use vocabulary terms to describe it to a partner.

Anya is buying a toy train. The price depends on the number of train cars.

Train Prices						
Number of Train Cars	1	2	3	4	5	6
Price	$5	$10	$15	$20		

Write a rule for the table. Then complete the table.

Rule: _____ .

Look at the number patterns. Write the rule. Then write the next number.

The rule is _____ .   The rule is _____ .

The next number is _____ .   The next number is _____ .

Talk About It
Complete the sentences about the patterns.

 The information about the train prices is given in a …

5 To find a rule for the table, I looked for a …

6 To find the next number in Problem 2, first I needed to find the …

7 The pattern in Problem 3 is **not** a …

Your Turn
Write a number pattern that follows a rule. Describe it to a partner. Use the sentence starters for support.

The pattern is …

The rule is …

Your Turn

Write the rule for each table. Complete each table.

1

Number of Markers	Number of Boxes
4	1
12	3
20	5
28	
36	

2

Price of Cheese Pizza	Price with 2 Toppings
$7	$10
$8	
$10	$13
$12	
$13	$16

Rule: _____ .

Rule: _____ .

3 Choose a rule from the box. Write a number pattern using the rule.

> add 5   subtract 5
> add 10   subtract 10

Pattern: _____, _____, _____, _____

Talk and Write About It

Complete the sentences about patterns.

Vocabulary

pattern	repeat	rule
repeating pattern	table	number pattern

4 To find the rule in each table, I looked for a _____ .

5 To make my pattern in Problem 3, I followed a _____ .

6 In the pattern 5, 1, 8, 5, 1, 8, 5, 1, 8, the _____ is 5, 1, 8.

Produce Language

Write the terms you learned about in this lesson in the third column of the chart on page 41. Write what you have learned about these terms. Use sentence starters from throughout the lesson for support.

Lines

Essential Question What terms do you need to know to understand and discuss lines?

You Will

- Recognize the properties of lines and line segments.
- Understand the relationship between pairs of lines.
- Use math vocabulary to describe lines.

Talk About It

Look at the list of terms below. In the first two columns of the chart, write terms you **know** or **want** to know more about.

line   intersecting lines
line segment   perpendicular lines
horizontal line   parallel lines
vertical line

Know	Want	Learned

Explain what you know about the terms you wrote in the chart. Use the sentence starters for help.

I know … means … in math.
I think … means …

Your Turn

Look at the objectives listed under You Will at the top of the page. Working with a partner, predict what you will learn. Use the sentence starter below.

I am going to learn about …

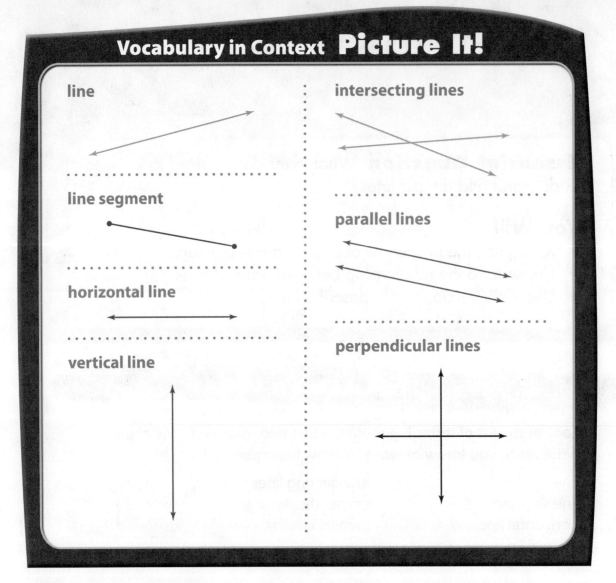

line

intersecting lines

line segment

parallel lines

horizontal line

perpendicular lines

vertical line

Talk About It

Talk with a partner to complete the sentences.

1. Part of a line that stops at each end is a ...

2. A line that goes across is a ...

3. A line that goes up and down is a ...

4. Lines that never cross are ...

Your Turn

Choose a term on this page. Draw three different examples of it. Show your drawings to a partner. Ask your partner to describe them.

On this map, Cedar Street and Rose Street look like perpendicular lines.

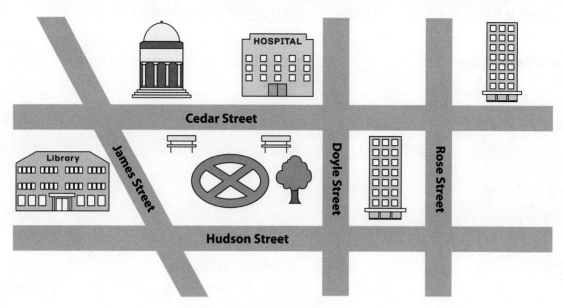

Map of Downtown

Use vocabulary terms to describe other streets on this map.

James Street and Cedar Street

_____

Doyle Street and Hudson Street

_____

Doyle Street and Rose Street

_____

Talk About It

Complete the sentences to help describe lines.

1 Lines that go across are …

2 Lines that never cross each other are …

3 Lines that cross each other are …

4 Lines that cross each other and form square corners are …

Your Turn

Draw two lines. Describe these lines to a partner using vocabulary terms.

Think, Talk, and Write

Your Turn

Draw a street map. Write a name on each street. Show streets that look like:

- intersecting lines
- perpendicular lines
- parallel lines

Write the names of a pair of streets that can be described by each term.

1. Intersecting lines: _____ and _____ .

2. Perpendicular lines: _____ and _____ .

3. Parallel lines: _____ and _____ .

Talk and Write About It

Complete the sentences about lines.

Vocabulary		
lines	horizontal lines	parallel lines
line segment	vertical lines	perpendicular lines
intersecting lines		

4. Lines that go up and down are _____ .

5. Part of a line that stops at each end is a _____ .

6. Lines that never intersect are _____ .

Produce Language

Write the terms you learned about in this lesson in the third column of the chart on page 45. Write about these terms. Use sentence starters from throughout the lesson for support.

Angles

Essential Question What vocabulary terms should you use to identify and describe angles?

You Will
- Identify and describe different types of angles.
- Recognize right angles, acute angles, and obtuse angles.
- Understand and use key terms related to angles.

Talk About It

Copy each term from Vocabulary in Context on a card. As your teacher reads each term, create three piles of cards.

1 Place terms that you know in **Pile 1.**

2 Place terms you have heard but are not sure what they mean in **Pile 2.**

3 Place terms you do not know in **Pile 3.**

What do you know about each term? Explain, using the sentence starters for support.

I know … means …
I think … means …
I do not know what … means.

angle

ray

vertex

Your Turn
Look at the objectives under You Will at the top of the page. Working with a partner, predict what you are going to learn. Use the sentence starter for support.

I am going to learn …

Vocabulary in Context **Picture It!**

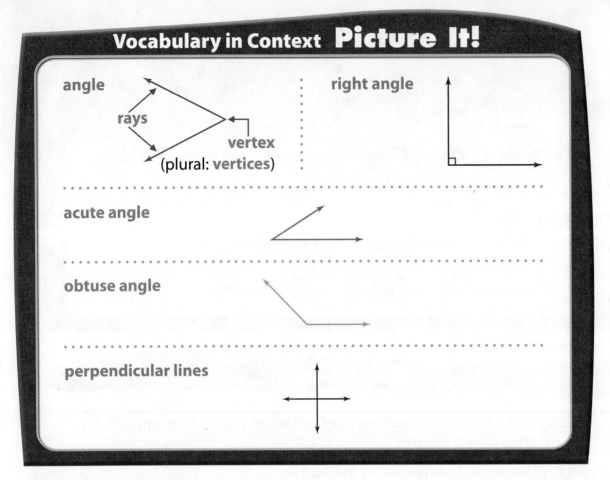

angle	right angle
rays	
vertex (plural: **vertices**)	
acute angle	
obtuse angle	
perpendicular lines	

Talk About It

Talk with a partner. Complete the sentences.

1. The point where the rays of an angle meet is the ...

2. An angle that opens less than a right angle is an ...

3. An angle that opens more than a right angle is an ...

4. Two lines that cross each other and form right angles are ...

Your Turn

Draw a right angle, an acute angle, and an obtuse angle. Under each angle, write the term that tells what kind of angle you drew. Write a sentence to describe each angle. Use the sentence starters for help.

This is a right angle because ...

This is an acute angle because ...

This is an obtuse angle because ...

Each corner of an index card is a right angle. You can use the card to go on an angle hunt. Move a corner of the card around the drawing of the castle to check for right angles. When you find a right angle, circle the vertex in red. Then look for acute and obtuse angles. Circle the vertices of acute angles in blue. Circle the vertices of obtuse angles in green.

Talk About It

What angles did you find? Complete the sentences to explain.

1. The angles that look like square corners are …

2. The angles that open less than a right angle are …

3. The angles that open more than a right angle are …

Your Turn

Use your index card to draw a pair of perpendicular lines.
Use vocabulary terms to explain to a partner why the lines are perpendicular.

Your Turn

Draw a picture in the space below. Include all three types of angles. Use red for the rays of a right angle. Use blue for the rays of an acute angle. Use green for the rays of an obtuse angle.

Talk and Write About It

Complete the sentences about angles.

> **Vocabulary**
>
> | | | |
> |---|---|---|
> | acute angle | obtuse angle | right angle |
> | rays | vertex | perpendicular lines |

1. Every angle is made up of two _____ .

2. Every angle has one _____ .

3. An angle that makes a square corner is a _____ .

4. Right angles can be formed by _____ .

Produce Language

Write about how the three types of angles are alike. Then write about how they are different. Use the sentence starters for help.

The angles are all formed by …

Right angles are different from acute angles because …

Shapes

Essential Question What words do you use when you discuss shapes?

You Will
- Identify and describe different types of shapes.
- Compare and contrast different types of shapes.
- Understand and use key terms that you need to give details about shapes.

Talk About It

Make an index card for each vocabulary term below. Place each card in one of three piles.

Pile 1: I know what this term means.
Pile 2: I have heard this term, but I am not sure how it is used in math.
Pile 3: I have not heard of this term.

Polygon

right angle	pentagon	square
circle	angle	triangle
quadrilateral	rectangle	vertex
hexagon	octagon	side
polygon		

What do you know about each term? Explain, using the sentence starters for support.

I know … means …
I think … means …
I do not know what … means.

Your Turn

Look at the objectives under You Will at the top of the page. Working with a partner, predict what you are going to learn. Use the sentence starter for support.

I am going to learn about …

Vocabulary in Context Picture It!

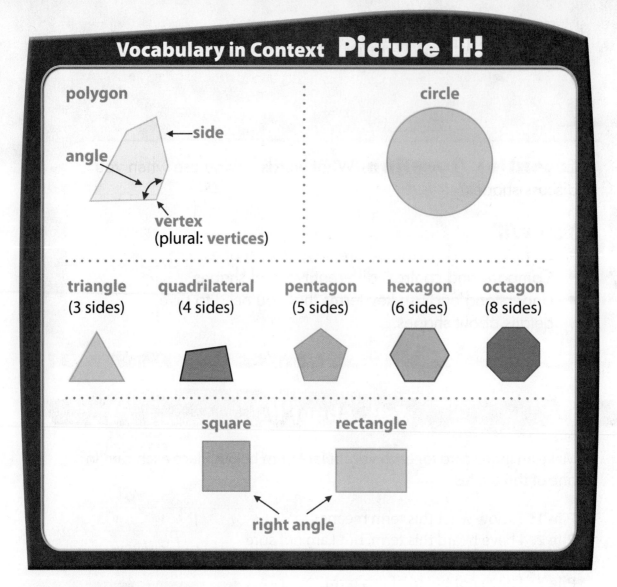

polygon

side

angle

vertex
(plural: vertices)

circle

triangle
(3 sides)

quadrilateral
(4 sides)

pentagon
(5 sides)

hexagon
(6 sides)

octagon
(8 sides)

square

rectangle

right angle

Talk About It

Talk with a partner. Complete the sentences.

1. Two sides of a polygon that meet form an …

2. A square has 4 … angles.

3. A triangle has 3 angles and 3 …

4. A … is not a polygon.

5. Since squares and rectangles have 4 sides, each one can also be called a …

Your Turn

Choose a shape to draw and describe. Use vocabulary terms in your description. Use them to label your drawing, too.

Draw a line from the name of each shape to the sign with that shape.
You might not find every shape.

octagon

circle

hexagon

pentagon

rectangle

square

triangle

Which shape did you **not** find? _____

Talk About It

How can you describe shapes? Complete the sentences to explain.

1 One shape that is not a polygon is a . . .

2 All 4 sides of a . . . are the same length.

3 The polygon with 3 sides is a . . .

4 Both a square and a . . . have 4 right angles.

5 An octagon has two more sides than a . . .

Your Turn

Write a few sentences to describe polygons. Give some examples. Use
the sentence starters for support. Share your ideas with a partner.

A polygon is . . .

One example of a polygon is . . .

It has . . . and . . .

Your Turn

These kites are all polygons. Fill in the chart to describe them.

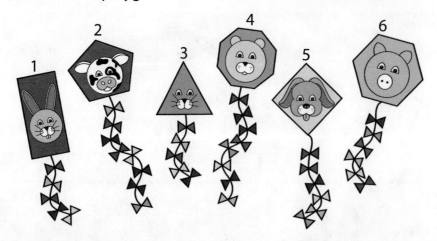

Kite	Type of Polygon	Number of Sides	Number of Angles
1			
2			
3			
4			
5			
6			

Talk and Write About It

Complete the sentences about shapes.

> **Vocabulary**
>
> right angle   triangle   square   hexagon
> pentagon   rectangle   circle   angle

7 A hexagon has twice as many sides as a _____ .

8 Each corner of a square is the vertex of a _____ .

9 A _____ has 5 sides .

Produce Language

Draw two polygons. Write sentences to describe each one.

Triangles and Quadrilaterals

Essential Question What vocabulary terms should you use to identify and describe triangles and quadrilaterals?

You Will
- Identify different types of triangles and quadrilaterals.
- Use key terms to describe triangles and quadrilaterals.

Talk About It

Look at the list of terms below. In the first two columns of the chart, write terms you **know** or **want** to know more about.

polygon	quadrilateral	trapezoid
acute triangle	rectangle	triangle
obtuse triangle	rhombus	scalene triangle
opposite sides	right triangle	isosceles triangle
parallel lines	square	equilateral triangle
parallelogram		

Know	Want	Learned

What do you know about each term? Explain, using the sentence starters for support.

I know … means …
I want to know more about …

Your Turn
Look at the objectives under You Will at the top of the page. Working with a partner, predict what you are going to learn. Use the sentence starter for support.

I am going to learn about …

Vocabulary in Context Picture It!

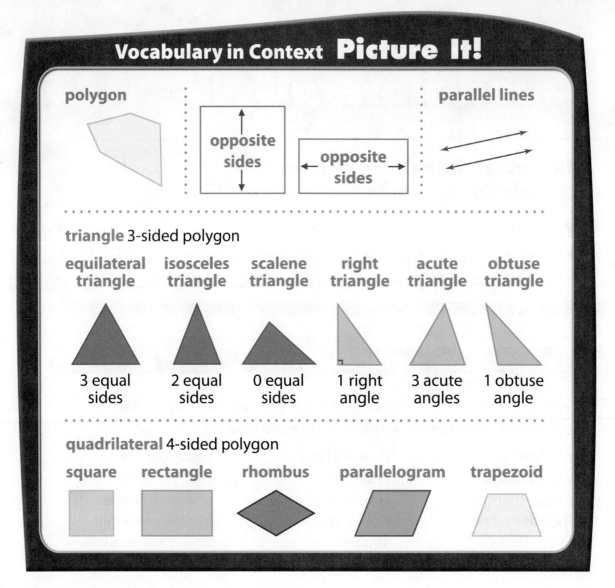

polygon

opposite sides

opposite sides

parallel lines

triangle 3-sided polygon

equilateral triangle	isosceles triangle	scalene triangle	right triangle	acute triangle	obtuse triangle
3 equal sides	2 equal sides	0 equal sides	1 right angle	3 acute angles	1 obtuse angle

quadrilateral 4-sided polygon

square	rectangle	rhombus	parallelogram	trapezoid

Talk About It

Talk with a partner. Complete the sentences.

1. A polygon with 3 sides is a ...
2. A polygon with 4 sides is a ...
3. Lines that never cross are ...
4. Sides that are across from each other are ...

Your Turn

Choose one quadrilateral and one triangle to draw and describe.
Use vocabulary terms in your descriptions. Use them to label your
drawings, too.

Look for polygons on the paper doll clothes. Draw a line from the polygon to the name of the polygon. The first one is done for you.

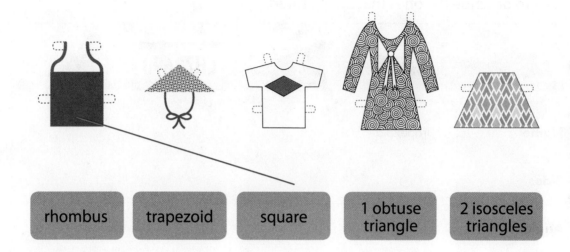

| rhombus | trapezoid | square | 1 obtuse triangle | 2 isosceles triangles |

Talk About It

How can you describe quadrilaterals and triangles? Complete the sentences to explain.

1. A polygon with 3 sides and 1 right angle is a …
2. A parallelogram is a kind of …
3. All three angles in an … are acute.
4. Both a square and a … have 4 equal sides.

Your Turn

Draw your own shirt for a paper doll. Use a quadrilateral or a triangle in your drawing. Write a few sentences to describe it. Use the sentence starters for support. Share your ideas with a partner.

Look for the … on this shirt.
This shape has … sides.
One of the angles is …

Think, Talk, and Write

Your Turn

You can see triangles and quadrilaterals all around you. Fill in the chart to describe the ones that are pictured.

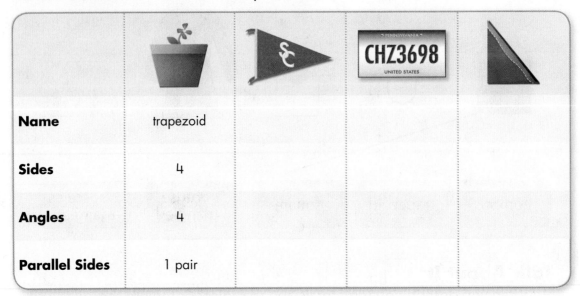

Name	trapezoid			
Sides	4			
Angles	4			
Parallel Sides	1 pair			

Draw an example of each polygon.

1. obtuse triangle
2. rhombus
3. parallelogram

Talk and Write About It

Complete the sentences about triangles and quadrilaterals.

Vocabulary

obtuse triangle	rectangle	right triangle	rhombus
parallelogram	quadrilateral	isosceles triangle	trapezoid
acute triangle	parallel lines	scalene triangle	square

4. A _____ has one right angle.

5. A trapezoid is a kind of _____ .

6. All angles are right angles in a square and in a _____ .

Produce Language

Write the terms you learned about in this lesson in the third column of the chart on page 57. Write what you have learned about these terms.

Figures in Our World

Essential Question How can you describe figures in the world around you?

You Will
- Identify shapes and solid figures.
- Understand and use key terms to describe and compare shapes and solid figures.

Talk About It

Rate these mathematical terms according to the following scale:

1 I do not know this term.

2 I have heard this term, but I do not know how to use it in math.

3 I understand this term and know how to use it in math.

____ shape	____ rectangle	____ cube
____ solid figure	____ rectangular prism	____ sphere
____ cone	____ pyramid	____ circle
____ vertex	____ figures	____ square
____ line of symmetry	____ edge	____ triangle
____ face	____ cylinder	____ symmetric figure

What do you know about each term? Explain, using the sentence starters for support.

I do not know what … means.
I think … means …
I know that … means …

Your Turn

Look at the objectives under You Will at the top of the page. Working with a partner, predict what you are going to learn. Use the sentence starter for support.

I am going to learn about …

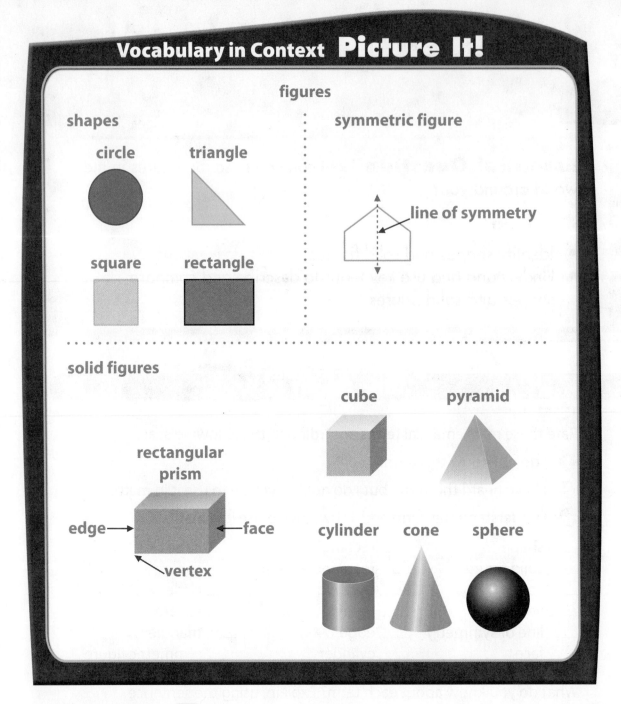

figures

shapes

circle   triangle

square   rectangle

symmetric figure

line of symmetry

solid figures

rectangular prism

edge → ← face

← vertex

cube   pyramid

cylinder   cone   sphere

Talk About It

Talk with a partner. Complete the sentences.

1 Triangles and circles are …

2 A shape that can be folded into two matching halves has a …

3 Cubes and pyramids are …

4 A solid figure shaped like a ball is a …

Your Turn

Choose a solid figure to describe. Use vocabulary terms.

You can see figures all around you. Look at the picture. Follow the directions to identify the figures.

1. Use red to circle these figures: sphere, triangle.

2. Use blue to circle these figures: rectangle, rectangular prism.

3. Use green to circle these figures: cylinder, cone.

4. Find a type of polygon that you have not circled. Use black to draw a line of symmetry on it.

Talk About It

How can you describe figures? Complete the sentences to explain.

5. A corner in a solid figure is called a …

6. The flat surface of a rectangular prism, cube, or pyramid is called a …

7. A figure shaped like a soup can is a …

Your Turn

Choose one figure from the picture and write a description. Use the sentence starters for support. Share with a partner. See if your partner can point to the right figure in the picture.

This figure is a …
It has …
It is called a …

Think, Talk, and Write

Your Turn

Draw a line from each picture to the type of figure it is.

circle

cylinder

rectangular prism

quadrilateral

sphere

triangle

Talk and Write About It

Complete the sentences about figures.

Vocabulary			
edge	line of symmetry	sphere	pyramid
face	rectangular prism	cone	cube
circle	square	cylinder	triangle

1 On a solid figure, an _____ is where two faces meet.

2 Each face of a cube is shaped like a _____ .

3 The flat part of a cone looks like a _____ .

Produce Language

Find one shape and one solid figure in the classroom. Describe them.

Units of Measure

Essential Question What do you need to know about the names of different units of measure?

You Will

- Identify customary and metric units of measure for length, weight or mass, and capacity.
- Determine the best units to use when measuring length, weight or mass, and capacity.
- Use the correct terms when discussing units of measure.

Talk About It

Copy each term from Vocabulary in Context on a card. As your teacher reads each term, create three piles of cards.

1. Place terms that you know in **Pile 1.**

2. Place terms you have heard but are not sure what they mean in **Pile 2.**

3. Place terms you do not know in **Pile 3.**

What do you know about each term? Explain, using the sentence starters for support.

I know … means …
I think … means …
I do not know what … means.

capacity

length

weight

Your Turn

Look at the objectives listed under You Will at the top of the page. Predict what you are going to learn. Use the sentence starter for support.

I am going to learn about …

Vocabulary in Context **Picture It!**

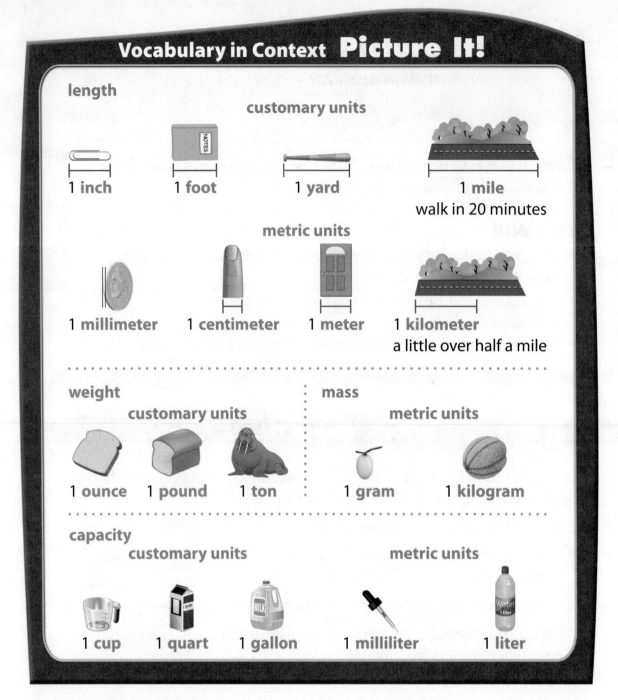

length

customary units

1 inch 1 foot 1 yard 1 mile
walk in 20 minutes

metric units

1 millimeter 1 centimeter 1 meter 1 kilometer
a little over half a mile

weight

customary units

1 ounce 1 pound 1 ton

mass

metric units

1 gram 1 kilogram

capacity

customary units

1 cup 1 quart 1 gallon

metric units

1 milliliter 1 liter

Talk About It

Talk with a partner. Complete the sentences.

1. Yards and inches are customary units of …
2. Liters and milliliters are … units of capacity.

Your Turn

Choose a unit of measure. Tell a partner what you could measure using
that unit.

Which is the better unit of measure? Circle the answer.

length

1 inch   yard   **2** kilometer   millimeter   **3** inch   foot

weight or mass

4 ounce   pound   **5** ton   ounce   **6** gram   kilogram

capacity

7 gallon   quart   **8** cup   gallon   **9** milliliter   liter

Talk About It

Which unit of measure should you use? Complete the sentences to explain.

10 To measure the length of a pencil, use inches or …

11 To measure the weight of a cell phone, use …

12 Use gallons to measure the … of a fish tank.

13 To measure the mass of a large dog, use …

14 Use feet, yards, or meters to measure the … of a school hallway.

15 Measure the capacity of an eye dropper using …

Your Turn

Choose two objects in your classroom. Write the units you would use to measure the length and weight of each.

Think, Talk, and Write

Your Turn

Tear out the Measurement Match activity on page 95.

Write the letter for the picture that could match the measures below.

weight		
_____	_____	_____
4 ounces	9 pounds	50 pounds

length		
_____	_____	_____
10 centimeters	20 yards	1 meter

capacity		
_____	_____	_____
3 cups	5 milliliters	10 gallons

Talk and Write About It

Complete the sentences about units of measure.

Vocabulary

centimeters	yards	grams	capacity
kilograms	pounds	inches	weight
metric units	mass	measure	length

1. To measure the length of a pen, use _____ .

2. A pound is a unit of _____ .

3. Centimeters and meters are _____ of length.

4. To measure mass, use _____ .

5. A liter is a metric unit of _____ .

6. A yard is a customary unit of _____ .

Produce Language

You want to know how tall you are. What is the best unit of measure to use? Explain why.

Measurement Tools

Essential Question How can you discuss measurement tools and what they measure?

You Will
- Identify measurement tools.
- Determine which tool to use to measure the length, the weight or mass, or the capacity of an object.
- Use key terms for units of measure and measurement tools.

Talk About It

Copy each term from Vocabulary in Context onto an index card. Place each card in one of three piles.

Pile 1: I know what this term means.
Pile 2: I have heard of this term, but I am not sure how it is used in math.
Pile 3: I have not heard of this term.

What do you know about each term?
Explain, using the sentence starters for support.

I know … means …
I have heard of … , but I don't know how to use it in mathematics.
I have not heard of …

Your Turn

Look at the objectives under You Will at the top of the page. Working with a partner, predict what you are going to learn. Use the sentence starter for support.

I am going to learn about …

length

ruler

INCHES												
0	1	2	3	4	5	6	7	8	9	10	11	12

Measures **inches** and **feet**

yardstick

INCHES
0 1 2 3 4 5 6 7 8 9 10 11 12 13 14 15 16 17 18 19 20 21 22 23 24 25 26 27 28 29 30 31 32 33 34 35 36

Measures inches, feet, and **yards**

meterstick

CM
0 10 20 30 40 50 60 70 80 90 100

Measures **centimeters** and **meters**

capacity	weight or mass
measuring cup	**pan balance**

Measures **cups, pints, quarts, milliliters,** and **liters**

Measures **ounces, pounds, grams,** and **kilograms**

Talk About It

Talk with a partner. Complete the sentences.

1. A measurement tool that measures weight or mass is a …

2. A tool that measures capacity is a …

3. A yardstick and a … are about the same length.

4. You can measure in inches, feet, and yards with a ruler or a …

Your Turn

Choose one measurement tool. Write about the tool and what it measures.

Choose the best tool for finding the measure listed. Draw a line from each measure to the tool.

1. length of this sheet of paper

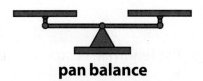

pan balance

2. length of your classroom

measuring cup

3. weight of a piece of cheese

ruler

4. capacity of a pot

meterstick

Talk About It

How do you know which measurement tool to use? Complete the sentences to explain.

5. You can measure length in inches with a yardstick or a …

6. To find the weight of this book, use a …

7. When you measure the amount of liquid in a pitcher, you are finding the pitcher's …

8. You can measure a pencil's mass with a …

9. To measure a rug's length, use a meterstick or a …

Your Turn

Choose a favorite pet or animal. Write the measurement tools you would use to measure its length and weight. Use the sentence starters for support.

My favorite animal is …
I need to see how many … long it is.
So, I would use a … to measure its length.
I need to see how many … it weighs.
So, I would use a … to measure its weight.

Think, Talk, and Write

Your Turn

Name the best tool and unit of measure for each object.

	Tool	Unit

1 the length in customary units _____ _____

2 the weight in customary units _____ _____

3 the capacity in metric units _____ _____

4 the length in metric units _____ _____

Talk and Write About It

Complete the sentences about measurement tools.

Vocabulary

mass	measuring cup	pan balance	feet
ruler	yardstick	meterstick	quart
weight	length	kilogram	capacity

5 A pan balance measures weight or _____ .

6 The best tool to measure the length of your thumb is a _____ .

7 Pints and quarts can be measured with a _____ .

8 The best tool to measure the height of a door is a meterstick

or a _____ .

Produce Language

You want to measure the length of your desk. What is the best
measurement tool to use? Explain why.

Perimeter and Area

Talk About It

Rate these mathematical terms according to the following scale.

1. I do not know this term.

2. I have heard this term, but I do not know how to use it in math.

3. I understand this term and I know how to use it in math.

_____ area   _____ square unit
_____ distance   _____ width
_____ length   _____ unit
_____ dimensions   _____ square inch
_____ perimeter   _____ square centimeter

Explain what you know about each term, using the sentence starters.

I do not know what … means.
I think … means …
I know … means … in math.

Your Turn

Look at the objectives under You Will at the top of the page. Working with a partner, predict what you are going to learn. Use the sentence starter for support.

I am going to learn about …

perimeter The **distance** around a shape

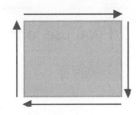

dimensions

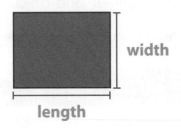

width

length

area The number of square units needed to cover a shape

1 unit   1 square unit

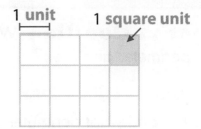

The area of the rectangle is 12 square units.

1 square centimeter   1 square inch

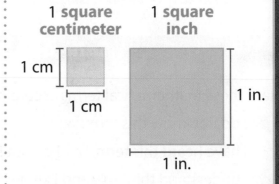

1 cm

1 cm

1 in.

1 in.

Talk About It

Talk with a partner. Complete the sentences.

1. The distance around a shape is its ...

2. The number of square units that fit inside a shape is its ...

3. When I find how far it is from my desk to the door, I am finding the ...

4. Length and width are ...

Your Turn

Describe *perimeter* and *area*. Use your own words and/or drawings. Share your description with a partner.

Cover this business card with 1-inch tiles from page 97. Find the perimeter and area.

1. How many tiles long is the card? _____ tiles

   What is the length of the card? _____ inches

2. How many tiles wide is the card? _____ tiles

   What is the width of the card? _____ inches

3. What is the perimeter of the card? _____ inches

4. How many tiles cover the card? _____ tiles

   What is the area of the card? _____ square inches

With the tiles, make a rectangle that has a perimeter of 12 inches. What is the area of this rectangle? _____

With the tiles, make a rectangle that has an area of 12 square inches. What is the perimeter of this rectangle? _____

Talk About It
Complete the sentences.

5. The distance around the card is its …

6. The number of inch tiles that cover the card is its …

7. To find the area of the card, count the tiles or multiply the … by the width.

Your Turn
Write how to find the perimeter and area of a square. Use the sentence starters for help. Share your ideas with a partner.

To find the perimeter of a square, you …
To find the area of a square, you …

Think, Talk, and Write

Your Turn

Draw the shapes described.

1 Draw a square with a perimeter of 16 units.

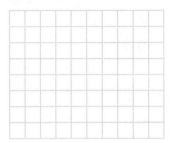

2 Draw a rectangle with an area of 20 square units.

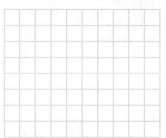

3 Draw a square with a perimeter of 24 units.

4 Draw a rectangle with an area of 18 square units.

Talk and Write About It

Complete the sentences about perimeter and area.

Vocabulary			
width	square units	area	length
perimeter	distance	dimensions	unit

5 The length and width of a figure are its _____ .

6 The distance around a figure is the _____ .

7 The area of a figure is given in _____ .

Produce Language

What is the difference between area and perimeter? Write about how they are different. You can include drawings as examples.

Time

Essential Question How do you use vocabulary terms to talk about telling time and the calendar?

You Will
- Tell time and talk about time using clocks.
- Use a calendar.
- Understand and use key terms related to time.

Talk About It

Work with a partner. Make an index card for each vocabulary term below. Place each card in one of three piles.

Pile 1: I know what this term means.
Pile 2: I have heard this term, but I am not sure how it is used in math.
Pile 3: I have not heard of this term.

hour hand	date	month
day	quarter	minute hand
calendar	hour	week
clocks	minutes	year
time		

What do you know about each term? Explain, using the sentence starters for support.

I know that … means …
I think … means …
I do not know what … means.

Your Turn

Look at the objectives under You Will at the top of the page. Working with a partner, predict what you are going to learn. Use the sentence starter for support.

I am going to learn about …

time on **clocks**

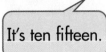

hour hand

minute hand

It's ten fifteen.

It's a quarter past ten.

60 **minutes** = 1 **hour**   24 hours = 1 **day**

calendar

month

days

date
March 8

weeks

S	M	T	W	T	F	S
				1	2	3
4	5	6	7	8	9	10
11	12	13	14	15	16	17
18	19	20	21	22	23	24
25	26	27	28	29	30	31

7 days = 1 week
Sunday, Monday, Tuesday,
Wednesday, Thursday,
Friday, Saturday

12 months = 1 **year**
January, February, March, April,
May, June, July, August, September,
October, November, December

Talk About It

Talk with a partner. Complete the sentences.

1. Look at a clock to see the …

2. There are 60 minutes in an …

3. Find a date on a …

4. Monday and Tuesday are days of the …

Your Turn

Tell what time it is now. Describe the time in two different ways.

Look at the clocks. Say the times to a partner. Then use numbers to write the times under the clocks.

_____   _____   _____

Look at the calendar. Label the parts.

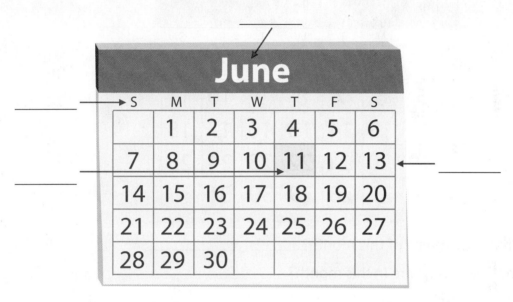

Talk About It

How do you talk about the time and the date? Complete the sentences to explain.

1. You tell the time in hours and …

2. June has 30 …

3. There are 7 days in 1 …

4. The day before Tuesday is …

Your Turn

What is today's date? Write sentences about today. Use the sentence starters for support. Share your ideas with a partner.

Today is …
There are … days in this month.

Think, Talk, and Write

Your Turn

Look at the clock. Answer the questions.

1. What is the time in numbers? _____

2. What is the time in words? _____

   _____

3. How many minutes are there in an hour? _____

Look at the calendar. Answer the questions.

May

S	M	T	W	T	F	S
			1	2	3	4
5	6	7	8	9	10	11
12	13	14	15	16	17	18
19	20	21	22	23	24	25
26	27	28	29	30	31	

4. What is the name of this month? _____

5. How many days are in this month? _____

6. What is the shaded date? _____

Talk and Write About It

Complete the sentences about clocks and calendars.

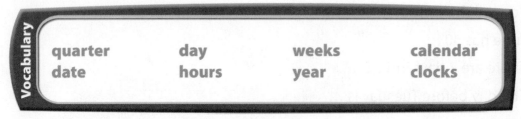

Vocabulary			
quarter	day	weeks	calendar
date	hours	year	clocks

7. A clock shows _____ and minutes.

8. A calendar shows 12 months of a _____ .

9. May 17 is a _____ .

Produce Language

Write about the day and the date of your birthday this year.

Collecting and Organizing Data

Essential Question What words should you use to discuss ways to collect and organize data?

You Will

- Identify some ways you can collect and organize data.
- Explain what a set of data shown in a chart means.
- Understand and use key terms related to collecting and organizing data.

Talk About It

Copy each term from Vocabulary in Context on a card. As your teacher reads each term, create three piles of cards.

1. Place terms that you know in **Pile 1.**
2. Place terms you have heard but are not sure what they mean in **Pile 2.**
3. Place terms you do not know in **Pile 3.**

What do you know about each term? Explain, using the sentence starters for support.

I know … means …
I think … means …
I do not know what … means.

survey

data

organize

Your Turn

Look at the objectives under You Will at the top of the page. Working with a partner, predict what you are going to learn. Use the sentence starter for support.

I am going to learn about …

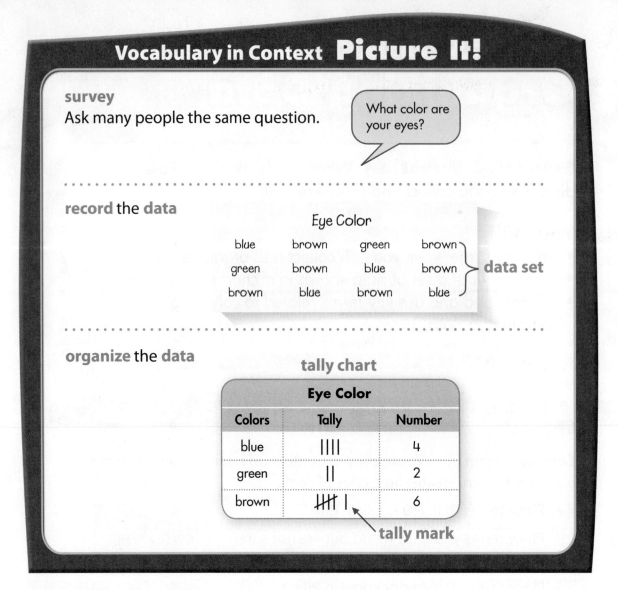

survey
Ask many people the same question.

What color are your eyes?

record the **data**

Eye Color

blue	brown	green	brown
green	brown	blue	brown
brown	blue	brown	blue

data set

organize the **data**

tally chart

Eye Color

Colors	Tally	Number
blue	IIII	4
green	II	2
brown	ШΗ I	6

tally mark

Talk About It

Talk with a partner. Complete the sentences.

1. You write tally marks in a …

2. Asking many people to name their favorite sport is one way to take a …

3. I record people's answers to make a …

4. A tally chart is a way to organize …

Your Turn

With a partner, explain how the data set was collected for the tally chart above. Explain what the tally chart shows.

Renda surveyed 12 people. She recorded the data. Finish the tally chart to organize Renda's data.

How Did You Get to School Today?			
Bus	Bus	Walk	Bus
Car	Bus	Car	Walk
Walk	Bus	Bus	Bus

Travel	Tally	Number

Answer the questions.

1. How many people get to school in a car? _____

2. How many people walk to school? _____

3. How do **most** people in the survey get to school? _____

Talk About It

How do you collect and organize data? Complete the sentences to explain.

4. Asking 12 people how they get to school is a …

5. The answers Renda recorded are the …

6. The tally chart has twelve …

Your Turn

What information would you like to find out? Write how you would collect and organize the data. Use the sentence starters for help. Share your ideas with a partner.

First I would …
To record the data, I would …
Then I would …

Your Turn

Survey 8 people. Ask: What is your favorite color?
Record the data. Then organize the data in the tally chart.

Favorite Color			

Favorite Color		
Color	Tally Marks	Number

Talk and Write About It

Complete the sentences about collecting and organizing data.

Vocabulary

survey	record	tally marks	organize
tally chart	data	data set	tally mark

1. I ask 8 people the same question to take a _____ .

2. The answers to the survey are called _____ .

3. You can organize the data in a _____ using tally marks.

Produce Language

Write the steps you followed to collect and organize the data about favorite colors.

Representing Data

Essential Question How can you talk about different types of graphs?

You Will
- Identify different types of graphs.
- Read graphs.
- Understand and use key terms related to graphs.

Talk About It

Look at the list of terms below. In the first two columns of the chart, write terms you **know** or **want** to know more about.

graph	symbol	scale
pictograph	bar graph	line graph
key	title	line plot

Know	Want	Learned

What do you know about each term? Explain, using the sentence starters for support.

I know … means …
I want to know more about …

Your Turn

Look at the objectives under You Will at the top of the page. Working with a partner, predict what you are going to learn. Use the sentence starter for support.

I am going to learn about …

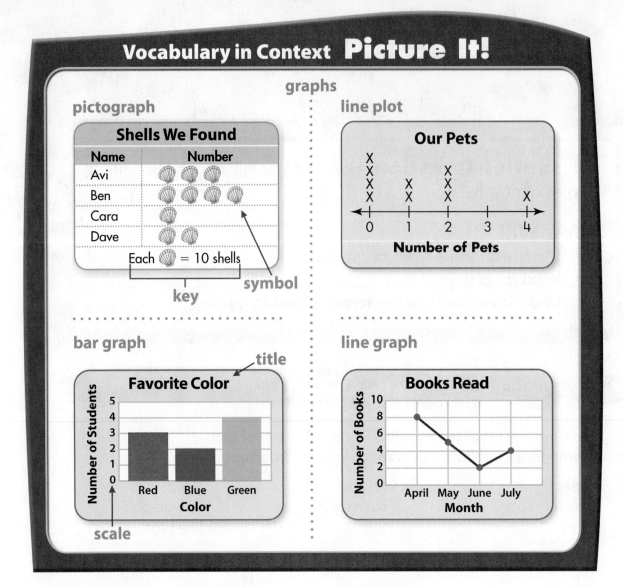

graphs

pictograph

Shells We Found

Name	Number
Avi	
Ben	
Cara	
Dave	

Each = 10 shells

key

symbol

line plot

Our Pets

Number of Pets

bar graph

title

Favorite Color

Number of Students / Color

scale

line graph

Books Read

Number of Books / Month

Talk About It

Talk with a partner. Complete the sentences.

1. A key tells how to read the symbols in a ...

2. In the line graph, the numbers 0, 2, 4, 6, 8, and 10 are the ...

3. "Our Pets" is the title of the ...

4. A graph that connects points with line segments is a ...

Your Turn

Describe one of the graphs above to a partner. Use the sentence starters for help.

The type of graph is ...
The title is ...

Write the name for each type of graph. Then answer the questions.

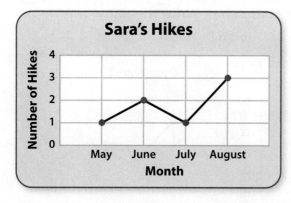

Sara's Hikes

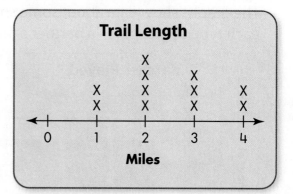

Trail Length

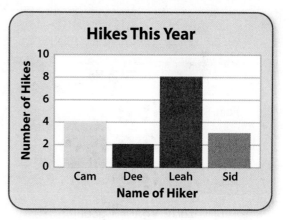

Miles Hiked

Maria	👢 👢 👢
Gary	👢 👢
Pedro	👢 👢 👢 👢
Val	👢

Each = 1 mile

Hikes This Year

1. Look at the line plot. How many trails are 2 miles?

2. Look at the bar graph. Who hiked the most?

3. Look at the pictograph. Who hiked 2 miles?

Talk About It

Complete the sentences about the graphs.

4. The numbers from 0 to 4 in the line graph are the …

5. Only the pictograph has a …

6. "Hikes This Year" is the … of the bar graph.

Your Turn

Choose two types of graphs to compare. Use the sentence starters for help. Share your ideas with a partner.

A … graph shows …
A … graph is different because …

Your Turn

The graphs show data about some soccer matches. Write the name for each type of graph. Tell a partner a fact about each graph.

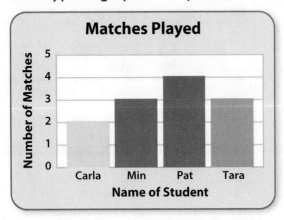

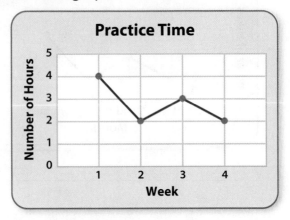

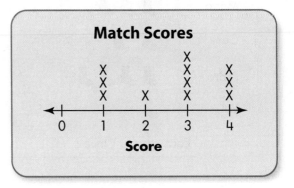

Match Scores

Talk and Write About It

Complete the sentences about graphs.

1. All of the graphs above have a _____ .

2. A graph that uses pictures or symbols is a _____ .

3. A graph that uses bars is called a _____ .

Produce Language

Write the terms you learned about in this lesson in the third column of the chart on page 85. Then write what you have learned about different kinds of graphs.

My Addition & Subtraction Words

Addition

add _____

plus (+) _____

sum _____

total _____

addend _____

_____

_____

_____

_____

Subtraction

subtract _____

minus (−) _____

difference _____

fewer than _____

left _____

_____

_____

_____

_____

My Multiplication & Division Words

Multiplication	Division
multiply	divide
times (X)	divided by (÷)
product	quotient
factors	divisor
array	dividend

Comparing Schools Four Corners Activity

Name of school _____

Number of students _____

Find a school on page 93 where the number of students **is less than** the number of students shown in this corner. Cut and paste that school here:

Name of school _____

Number of students _____

Find a school on page 93 where the number of students **is greater than** the number of students shown in this corner. Cut and paste that school here:

Comparing Schools Four Corners Activity

Corner 3

Name of school _____

Number of students _____

Find a school on page 93 where the number of students **is equal to** the number of students shown in this corner. Cut and paste that school here:

Corner 4

Name of school _____

Number of students _____

Draw a small picture of **your** school here:

Ask your teacher how many students attend your school.

Write that number here: _____

Is that number **less than, greater than,** or **equal to** the number of students shown in this corner? _____

Comparing Schools Four Corners Activity Cards

Cut out each card. Then follow the directions on pages 91–92.

Hemingway School
225 students

Buckley School
185 students

Lincoln School
322 students

Dante School
566 students

Morgan School
322 students

Nelson School
207students

Adams School
154 students

Copernicus School
300 students

Glenn School
179 students

Measurement Match

weight

A   B   C

length

D   E   F

capacity

G   H   I

Inch Tiles

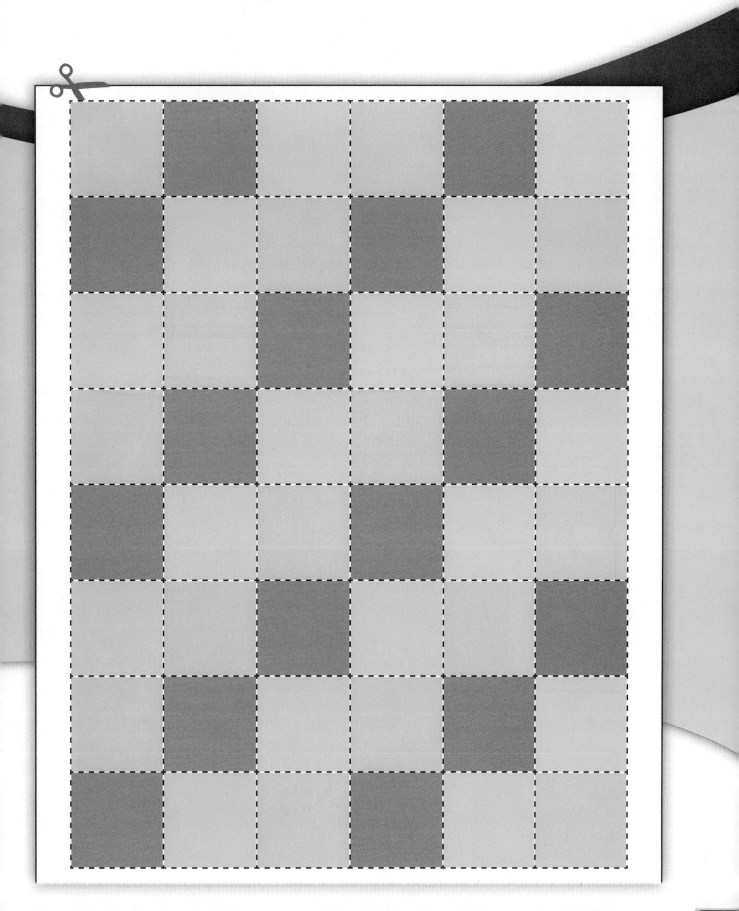

ISBN-13: 978-0-13-317288-1
ISBN-10:   0-13-317288-0

PEARSON

3